WILLIAM WALTON
arr. Tom Winpenny

SPITFIRE PRELUDE AND FUGUE

OXFORD

Spitfire Prelude and Fugue

from *The First of the Few*

WILLIAM WALTON
(1902–83)
arr. Tom Winpenny

Prelude

Sw.: Reeds 8', 4'
Gt.: Prin. 8', 4', 2', Sw. to Gt.
Ped. Prin. 16' 8', Sw. to Ped., Gt. to Ped.

This arrangement was performed at the conclusion of the Service to Commemorate the 75th Anniversary of the Battle of Britain at St Paul's Cathedral, London, by Peter Holder on 15 September 2015. It has been recorded on the Regent and Priory labels.

poco allarg.　　　　　　　　　　　a tempo

Fugue

* Small notesheads indicate optional pedal notes.

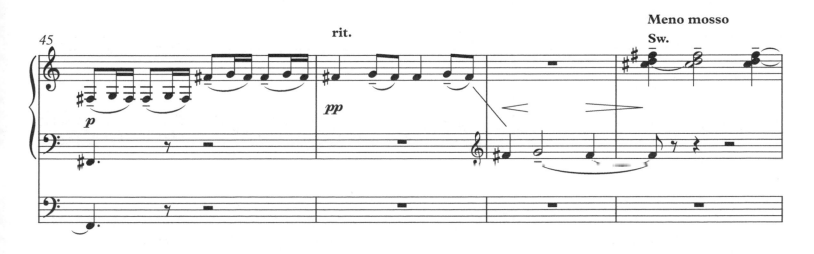

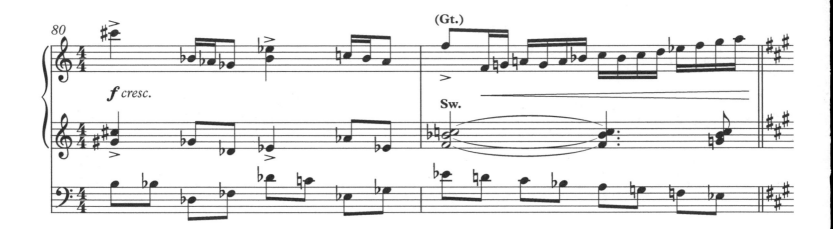

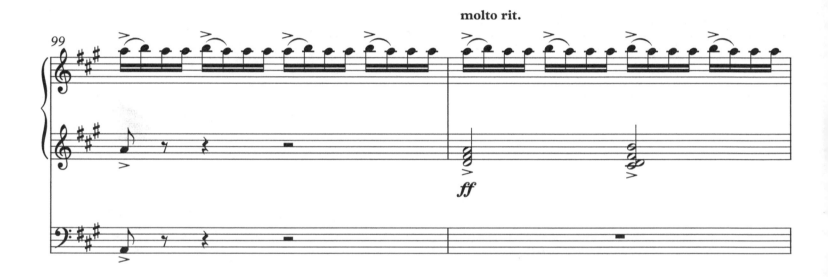